CRICKET’S PURE P

the story of an extraordinary match:

Middlesex v. Yorkshire, September 2015

by Tim Cawkwell

SFORZINDA BOOKS, Norwich, UK

set in Book Antiqua 12 pt

FOREWORD

This book is an account in words and images of a single cricket match. Besides the pleasure of the game, I had the pleasure of the company of Stephen Adamson on the first day, and of Jonathan Hourigan and Charles Rees on the second. Another pleasure was being at Lord's Cricket Ground for four days for which the MCC must take the credit. In this modest venture I have received encouragement and help from Charles Barr, who besides being an expert on British cinema, is very well-versed both in the history of the game and in the literature of cricket. It was he who suggested I approach Stephen Chalke of Fairfield Books and himself a writer on cricket, from whom I received valuable advice. Finally, while the words on Bentham's pleasure principle are entirely my own, I did make use of the Wikipedia entry on the 'felicific calculus'.

The photographs were taken with a Nikon Coolpix S6400.

Tim Cawkwell, Norwich, UK

"Walk about Sion, and go round about her. . .

Consider her palaces, that ye may tell them that come after."

The game of cricket grew out of the countryside, some mythological English landscape, outside of time. From the beginning it avoided being frantic, surely? In the 21st century the newer versions of the game have become so – and are having the effect of revivifying the game with six-hitting, faster and faster centuries, and Test Matches over in three days. This is not to be scorned, but neither is the contemplative version of cricket over four or five days, where the accumulation of performances is so important.

Other games aspire to length: athletics at the Olympics are a three-week event in which performance needs to be sustained and capped; tennis championships test the players over several contests not just one; this is also true of football's World Cup and other big-tournament events, and in its way of league football, rugby, basketball, whatever, where ultimate victory is the result of several victories. But the players in these sports get a rest between their exertions. Only golf tournaments spread over four days come close to cricket in their cumulative intensity, and the sporting event that comes closest to long-game cricket is golf's Ryder Cup played every other year between Europe and the USA. It lasts three days between teams of twelve, and the twelve singles matches on the last day involve all the players. Yet, for the most part, golf is played in a single person's mind, whereas cricket needs to be played not just in the individual mind and with individual skills but in the collective mind of the team: to win everyone must contribute, the whole must be greater than the sum of the personal contributions, and that collective mind must be sustained over several days. If one puts the Ryder Cup on one side, that makes long cricket unique among world sports.

At the start of 2015 it was a new-year resolution of mine to attend if I could a complete match in the county championship. The weather forecast was going to be important, and finding a good match to watch in which much would be at stake. I had therefore to bide my time until the summer to see which teams were making the running, and then to check the forecast weather to find a match with a reasonable chance of being played right through. Another virtue of county cricket helped: because it attracts a small audience, a ticket bought on the day is guaranteed.

Sidebottom, in touching distance when he retired to the outfield on Day 3, hardly needs his name on his shirt, for his locks identify him instantly.

As the year wore on, one fixture in particular came into focus: Middlesex v Yorkshire scheduled for 9 to 12 September, to be played at Lord's. As it turned out, this was the needle match for the county championship: the top side, Yorkshire, against the side placed second, Middlesex, with only a fixture or two remaining after that. It began with a triple-wicket maiden from Yorkshire's Ryan Sidebottom in the opening over, putting the result beyond contention. He was batting right at the end too – on the losing side.

The whole three-and-a-half days were a fine advertisement for the long game, for its vicissitudes, for its slow-motion evolution, for its thrilling surprises.

I would like to boast that I saw every ball, except that I got the 8.30 from Norwich (the 8.00 was significantly more expensive), consoling myself with the thought that the opening overs would not produce much action. Play having started at 10.30, I arrived at Lord's around 10.50. While Steve got some coffee, in my eagerness not to miss a ball I ran up some stairs to watch – and saw Sidebottom running in to bowl and having Eskinazi caught by Lyth at first slip. And then I saw the scoreboard: 14-4. So much for a quiet opening. It flashed through my mind that the pleasure of absorbing myself in four days of cricket was about to be curtailed, reduced to three days if not two.

Middlesex were all out for 106 – so no batting points and three bowling points to Yorkshire, so that the championship was virtually theirs. At 3.06 p.m. news came through that Nottinghamshire had not secured enough batting points to keep their trophy challenge alive –

so Yorkshire had won the championship and looked to be cruising to victory. Did this cause Yorkshire to relax? The Middlesex fightback started on Day 1 as they too found life in the pitch: at the end of the day Yorkshire were nine wickets down and only 120 or so runs ahead. A Yorkshire victory was certainly in the realm of probability but not in the realm of certainty that I had entered in my own mind at 10.50 that morning. On the other hand I was convinced that the game could not go on longer than two-and-a-half days.

Day 2 had started well for Yorkshire when the last wicket pair of Brooks and Sidebottom added some 60 runs, so they were 299 all out, 193 ahead on the first innings. The result still could not be in doubt. Although Middlesex then batted steadily through the day, repairing some damage, they were surely heading for defeat on Day 3 – succumbing to quick wickets and then Yorkshire knocking off the runs.

It was Day 3 that saw the real turn-round: Compton made 149, Franklin 63, Simpson 47 (from 194 balls, a pleasantly funereal rate, not a negligible contribution to his team since it caused the bowlers to doubt themselves). What is more, in the last hour or two the 9 and 10 batsmen had a partnership of 146, with Toby Roland-Jones clubbing his way to 103 (off 144 balls), 10 of them in the last over of the day courtesy of Leaning's modest tweaks. Was this a sporting gesture from the Yorkshire captain, allowing Roland-Jones to reach his century, or a way of prompting Middlesex to declare on 573? This they did overnight, leaving themselves a day to get 10 wickets, and a run chase for Yorkshire of 381 at 4.76 an over.

On Day 4 it was definitely advantage Middlesex, and they seized it. Yorkshire set off for the total but when Gale, batting at number 4, went in the 36th over with 92 on the board, the task of winning was beyond them. Would it be worth battling for a draw? I think they thought to themselves it was not, even if in the dressing room no such sentiments were articulated. The option of a draw feels like a poor one when vital points are not at stake, lacking in entertainment value, and ending in a result that feels closer to a defeat than to a victory. Although they had won or drawn all their 2015 county championship games up to that point, and a victory at Lord's was a sweet target, yet when it did not present itself, they subsided.

After all, they were already champions. The stage was set for the afternoon session when Roland-Jones took 5 for 27 starting with the principal stumbling-block, Lees. When at 106 he went for 62 runs resistance seemed to cease, and they ended up 134 all out, Middlesex winning by 246 runs.

There is one statistic that looks very odd: Day 1 saw nineteen wickets fall, Day 2 six wickets, Day 3 three wickets, Day 4, between the hours of 10.00 a.m. and 3 p.m., ten wickets.

What was afoot here? Yorkshire knew the pitch would help them on the first day, so having won the toss they opted to field, a decision thoroughly vindicated by what transpired in the opening session. However, from the stands, batting conditions looked reasonably benign, and the second and third days, played in bright sunlight, seemed to confirm this. On the last day of the match, Middlesex extracted pace and bounce. Yet more pertinent was the sense that the game was theirs: bowl tightly, take catches, field with attack – and victory would follow. The secondary means to that end were harnessed to the primary will to win. Chance helps those who help themselves.

Was this the most remarkable reversal ever in a cricket match? Stephen Chalke, author of 'Summer's Crown: the story of cricket's County Championship', pointed out to me that in his view it was the "the second greatest turnaround in the history of the County Championship", the first being Somerset's victory over Yorkshire at Headingley in 1901. That three-day game went like this: Somerset 87 all out; Yorkshire 325 all out; Somerset 630 all out; Yorkshire 113 all out. Somerset won by 279 runs. Again, a marked A-B-B-A structure, what a rhetorician would call 'chiastic', with even more startling scores than in the match I witnessed. Or was it rather the game Charles Barr steered me to, Warwickshire v. Hampshire at Edgbaston in 1922, again over three days? Warwickshire made 223, then bowled Hampshire out for 15 (Howell 6 wickets for 7 runs, Calthorpe 4 for 4). Game over? Following on, Hampshire then made 521 - and bowled Warwickshire out for 158. Game over. (There is a marvellous account of this match at www.cricketweb.net/the-greatest-comeback-in-history.)

There is no more ephemeral fact than sporting victory, although the sensation of it lingers in the mind. I had only seen at first hand one long game of cricket before: India versus England in Mumbai in 2006 which resulted in an England victory. That was deeply satisfying at the time, but the memory of that game is composed of numerous other things more vivid than the pleasure of the side winning that I wanted to win: Tendulkar making batting look simple, an excruciatingly slow half-century from Flintoff (brilliant in its way), Panesar dropping a catch which prompted an Indian spectator to remark, "Come on, Monty, do it for England," and so on. Not to mention shenanigans with the replay screen which was closed down on the second day because the operators chose to second-guess the third umpire and flash the results of appeals before the official announcement. This was a curious version of justice, to punish the spectators for the transgressions of the scoreboard operators. The administrators stumbled badly I thought, but their compatriots made up for it: when the game ended, the Indian spectators among whom we were sitting gave a courteous handshake and uttered polite congratulations. I was touched, and still am to this day.

In 2015, when play finished on Day 4, my predominant feeling, which time is not going to erase, was how miraculous to have witnessed in person the whole of such an exceptional game on only the second time of choosing to watch every ball of a long game, in contrast to football fans who watch their team week in, week out, waiting for the exceptional win that makes all the other defeats bearable and regularly being denied. Admittedly on this occasion, I had no investment in the result, as I would have been as happy with a Yorkshire win as I was with a Middlesex one. All I wanted was good cricket, not necessarily exciting but hard-played, and this was what I got: over four days, 38 wickets and 1,112 runs, no play lost to rain, maybe an over or two to bad light at the end of the first day – a champagne picnic short of a cucumber sandwich? For four days I lived in slow motion of an intense kind.

Match details

Yorkshire won toss and chose to field

Result Middlesex won by 246 runs

Umpires SJ O'Shaughnessy and RT Robinson

Close of play

Day 1 Yorkshire 1st innings 238-9

Day 2 Middlesex 2nd innings 274-5

Day 3 Middlesex 2nd innings 573-8

Day 4 Yorkshire 2nd innings 134 all out

SCORECARD

Middlesex 1st innings

PR Stirling	lbw b Sidebottom	0
SD Robson	c Lees b Bresnan	26
NRD Compton	c Hodd b Sidebottom	0
DJ Malan	b Sidebottom	0
SS Eskinazi	c Lyth b Sidebottom	4
NJ Dexter	c Hodd b Bresnan	18
JEC Franklin*	c Leaning b Bresnan	12
JA Simpson†	c Hodd b Middlebrook	28
JAR Harris	not out	9
TS Roland-Jones	lbw b Bresnan	0
TJ Murtagh	b Sidebottom	3
Extras	(lb 4, nb 2)	6
Total	(all out; 33 overs)	**106** (3.21 runs per over)

Fall of wickets 1-0 (Stirling, 0.3 ov), 2-0 (Compton, 0.5 ov), 3-0 (Malan, 0.6 ov), 4-14 (Eskinazi, 4.5 ov), 5-44 (Dexter, 12.5 ov), 6-55 (Robson, 18.3 ov), 7-92 (Simpson, 25.6 ov), 8-95 (Franklin, 29.3 ov), 9-95 (Roland-Jones, 29.6 ov), 10-106 (Murtagh, 32.6 ov)

Bowling

RJ Sidebottom	12-5-18-5
JA Brooks	6-0-39-0
SA Patterson	6-2-11-0
TT Bresnan	8-1-30-4
JD Middlebrook	1-0-4-1

Yorkshire 1st innings

A Lyth	lbw b Roland-Jones	25
AZ Lees	lbw b Stirling	39
GS Ballance	lbw b Roland-Jones	0
AW Gale*	c Robson b Dexter	98
JA Leaning	lbw b Dexter	9
TT Bresnan	lbw b Dexter	11
AJ Hodd†	b Murtagh	20
JD Middlebrook	c Simpson b Roland-Jones	4
SA Patterson	c Simpson b Murtagh	0
JA Brooks	not out	50
RJ Sidebottom	c&b Murtagh	28
Extras	(b 2, lb 1, w 2, nb 10)	15
Total	(all out; 72 overs)	**299** (4.15 runs per over)

Fall of wickets 1-45 (Lyth, 9.2 ov), 2-51 (Ballance, 11.2 ov), 3-129 (Lees, 28.3 ov), 4-163 (Leaning, 36.1 ov), 5-187 (Bresnan, 40.6 ov), 6-198 (Gale 44.2 ov), 7-217 (Hodd, 48.5 ov), 8-217 (Patterson, 50.3 ov), 9-221 (Middlebrook, 51.1 ov), 10-299 (Sidebottom, 71.6 ov)

Bowling

TJ Murtagh	18-1-81-3
TS Roland-Jones	25-5-93-3
JAR Harris	12-0-67-0
JEC Franklin	5-1-18-0
PR Stirling	4-1-13-1
NJ Dexter	8-2-24-3

Middlesex 2nd innings

SD Robson	b Bresnan	53
PR Stirling	b Middlebrook	34
NRD Compton	lbw b Middlebrook	149
DJ Malan	lbw b Middlebrook	0
SS Eskinazi	b Patterson	22
NJ Dexter	c&b Brooks	13
JEC Franklin*	lbw b Sidebottom	63
JA Simpson†	lbw b Lyth	47
JAR Harris	not out	67
TS Roland-Jones	not out	103
Extras	(b 6, lb 8, nb 8)	22
Total	(8 wickets dec; 175 overs)	**573** (3.27 runs per over)
Did not bat	TJ Murtagh	

Fall of wickets 1-87 (Robson, 23.1 ov), 2-87 (Stirling, 24.3 ov), 3-87 (Malan, 24.6 ov), 4-128 (Eskinazi, 41.2 ov), 5-143 (Dexter, 46.2 ov), 6-293 (Franklin, 84.3 ov), 7-380 (Compton, 118.1 ov), 8-427 (Simpson, 136.1 ov)

Bowling

RJ Sidebottom	28-7-70-1
JA Brooks	27-3-122-1
SA Patterson	33-8-96-1
TT Bresnan	37-13-108-1
JD Middlebrook	40-7-130-3
A Lyth	8-0-19-1
JA Leaning	2-0-14-0

Yorkshire 2nd innings (target: 381 runs)

A Lyth	c Simpson b Harris	14
AZ Lees	c Malan b Roland-Jones	62
GS Ballance	c Simpson b Harris	0
AW Gale*	lbw b Dexter	17
JA Leaning	c Robson b Roland-Jones	4
TT Bresnan	c Simpson b Harris	9
AJ Hodd†	c Simpson b Roland-Jones	0
JD Middlebrook	c Malan b Roland-Jones	0
SA Patterson	b Murtagh	9
JA Brooks	c Eskinazi b Roland-Jones	2
RJ Sidebottom	not out	6
Extras	(lb 7, nb 4)	11
Total	(all out; 58 overs)	**134** (2.31 runs per over)

Fall of wickets 1-28 (Lyth, 12.4 ov), 2-28 (Ballance, 12.6 ov), 3-92 (Gale, 36.4 ov), 4-106 (Lees, 41.3 ov), 5-111 (Leaning, 47.2 ov), 6-111 (Hodd, 47.3 ov), 7-115 (Bresnan, 48.5 ov), 8-115 (Middlebrook, 49.2 ov), 9-117 (Brooks, 51.6 ov), 10-134 (Patterson, 57.6 ov)

Bowling

TJ Murtagh	7-3-18-1
TS Roland-Jones	21-10-27-5
JAR Harris	14-6-37-3
JEC Franklin	4-2-7-0
PR Stirling	4-2-7-0
NJ Dexter	8-2-31-1

DAY 1: battle truly joined. By the time I had deployed my camera to engage with the action, the Middlesex first innings was over and Yorkshire were batting. On the left, Murtagh bowls at the opener, Adam Lyth. Below, Middlesex attack with three slips and a gully set back for the mistimed drive.

As I sat directly beneath the media centre, a mysterious helicopter appeared and hovered overhead in the late afternoon.

The loneliness of the long game: umpires (left) and first slip (below).

Yorkshire 158 for 3 at 4.30 in the afternoon.

End of Day 1 on an apocalyptic note.

DAY 2: bright and sunny, good weather for batting, it seemed. Middlesex did badly to get skittled out on the first day, but did well in carrying out their own exercise in skittling. If they could get the last Yorkshire wicket, they had time to repair the damage.

I was joined for the day by Jonathan and Charles, whom I know as Bressonians – that is, aficionados of the films of the Frenchman Robert Bresson. The batsmen had plenty of time; so did we to analyse the unfolding match, using reason and speculation in predicting what might happen. But we also talked about the forthcoming Frank Auerbach exhibition, using reason and speculation as to what this might be like.

Discussion of painting moved on to the cinema. The scene before us was very English, and since time was not of the essence, and as the game took its leisurely course, one of us raised the question of what were our desert-island British films, assuming of course that the island came equipped with a cinema. My choice was a quick delivery of a full length: Hitchcock's *Blackmail*, Powell and Pressburger's *A Canterbury Tale*, and – here I got the ball cleverly to seam away at the end – Mike Leigh's *Mr Turner*. Charles bowled a yorker on the middle stump: Humphrey Jennings' *Listen to Britain*, Hitchcock's *The Lady Vanishes*, and Robert Hamer's *Kind Hearts and Coronets*. Then it was Jonathan's turn: Powell and Pressburger's *I Know Where I'm Going* – the ball is on a perfect length; Terence Davies' *Distant Voices, Still Lives* – the ball starts rising; Lean and Coward's *This Happy Breed* – the ball is swerving sharply; Bruce Robinson's *Withnail and I* – the ball strikes the helmet with a resounding clang. As we weighed these offerings, we realised we had not bowled the Carol Reed ball (*The Third Man*) nor the more obvious David Lean one (*Brief Encounter*, which Bresson had called 'admirable'). Jonathan mused about bowling a few gentle Roeg tweaks: *Bad Timing, Don't Look Now, Walkabout*. In general, the choices showed our age, but then they showed knowledge too and a taste for films from the classical period and for an absence of modern mannerism, in harmony with our pleasure in the long game of cricket.

Just as a whole day gives time for conversation, four days give time for the slow vicissitudes of fortune to reveal themselves. Middlesex began to get a toehold in the game, ending the day on 270 for five wickets, with Nick Compton proving the rock on which the innings was being built, 86 not out.

The magnificent six stride out at the end of the Yorkshire 1st innings: the ground staff.

Middlesex 2nd innings: quality on display. Tim Bresnan (23 Tests for England) bowls at Sam Robson (7 Tests for England).

In the late afternoon, the descending sun endowed the pates of the members in the top tier of the pavilion with a small halo of light, as if this was a vision of the souls of the righteous in heaven.

Left: Sidebottom to Franklin.
Above: close of play score on Day 2, with Middlesex on 274 for 5, Compton 86 not out, Franklin 60 not out.

DAY 3: a blissful day of September sunshine. I basked in it, revolving themes in my mind: could I have improved my choice of films? I didn't think so, on reflection. Where should I sit? I chose the front of the lower grandstand in order to enjoy the sun to the full. Would Yorkshire roll over Middlesex and send me back to Norwich a day earlier than I had intended? Yes, surely. Middlesex were 78 runs ahead, with only five wickets in hand.

Being on my own, I had time to gaze. At around 11.00 a.m. a bird of prey was visible circling then skimming off sideways above the Mound and Tavern stands. My brain was idle: a sparrowhawk was my first thought, then a peregrine (there are over two dozen pairs in London now), and then I reverted to sparrowhawk as being most likely. My birdwatching brain was not in gear, if it could not tell a hawk from a falcon, *accipiter* from *falco.* The line from Hamlet came to mind: "When the wind is southerly, I know a hawk from a handsaw." Either the wind was not southerly or my mind wasn't.

Another ineluctable conundrum to surface in my mind was this: the ground looked empty but it did not feel empty. The best crowd was on the first day in which I guessed the Yorkshire supporters outnumbered the Middlesex ones, drawn by the prospect of being present when Yorkshire won the County Championship. The audience thinned in the next two days, but neither did it return in numbers for the fourth day when Middlesex was poised for a remarkable victory. What is more that was a Saturday, albeit in the football season. Throughout, the decibel level was low, and an unsystematic glance around those present showed there was virtually no-one there under 30.

In the meantime the batting continued. . .

Nick Compton goes on and on.

James Middlebrook retired last year but was then drafted for 2015 by Yorkshire as short-term cover. He took 17 wickets in the season, and won a championship medal. He is 38 years old, but still danced to the wicket.

Yorkshire, led by their wicketkeeper, Andy Hodd, appeal for lbw, without success. Ryan Sidebottom at square leg has no comment to make.

Not a pitch invasion: at the lunch interval we were allowed to tour the outfield. It turned out to be the Elysian Fields.

"Middlesex is now on Instagram," the scoreboard read. Below is a picture of the Instagram generation.

Old Father Time measures 'time not our time', in TS Eliot's phrase, measuring the seconds, stretching the minutes, holding back the hours.

The weariness of the long-distance fast bowler: Ryan Sidebottom (left) who ended the season top of the bowling averages.

The patience of the long-distance captain: Andrew Gale (right), the irresistible force, ponders how to shift the immovable rock of Nick Compton (centre), still going on.

Old Father Groundsman and broom-wielding acolyte retire after conducting the mysteries of wicket maintenance.

It is 4 p.m. on Day 3, and Middlesex have been batting for some 150 overs, when their 1st innings had lasted for 33.

The long game is wonderfully suited to the philosophic spectator, who has ample time to reflect: why, for example, do batsmen find half-century and century milestones tricky to negotiate? Is it chance they fall then, or destiny of some kind? Since cricket is played with mind as well as body, they render themselves vulnerable. Gale was out on 98 (Day 1), while Compton was out on 149 and Simpson on 47 (both Day 3).

Why do fielders drop catches? Roland-Jones was dropped in the outfield on his way to his hundred, when getting this ninth wicket would have given Yorkshire a real chance of victory. The explanation is simple: the fielder was Sidebottom, 37 years old, and compelled to go for an awkward catch when he had been bowling and fielding all day. It was perfectly human for him to err; you could almost say he was entitled to do so. The spirit was sufficiently willing, the flesh, reasonably enough, too weak.

These ruminations took place not against silence, but against an amiable ambient noise provided by the indistinct murmuration of the modest crowd. But there were two very audible interruptions, both to the point. The first was when Middlesex reached 529 just after 5.00 p.m. on Day 3. The resident announcer enunciated in the plummiest of accents that you only find at Lord's: "Ladies and Gentlemen, 528 represents the highest score by Middlesex against Yorkshire" – pause, then astonishment (mild), then clapping (also mild) – "beating 527 scored at Huddersfield in 1887, in the reign of Queen Victoria." Cue laughter. The second interruption was during the last session of the day when an anonymous shout, not in a Lord's accent, broke the polite reverie: "C'mon Yorkshire, you're champions, get 'em out."

A further pleasure had been the opportunity to watch two true competitors. Nick Compton is 32 and might have reflected that his brilliant future was behind him: games for England in 2012 and 2013, then dropped. But for Middlesex in the 2015 season he scored 1,123 runs in 31 innings, at an average of 38.7. His ability to apply himself must have been in the selectors' mind when he was chosen to tour South Africa in the winter of 2015/16, and a score of 149 against the County Champions to resurrect his side must have especially caught their eye. Secondly, another part-time England player and full-time star of the county circuit was Ryan Sidebottom who finished the season top of the bowling averages with 41 wickets at an average of 17.9. (As if this was not enough, he was also tenth in the batting averages.) What other bowler can savour three wickets in an opening maiden over?

DAY 4: Middlesex declared overnight at 573, a terrific achievement that had batted Yorkshire into a position of submission, and batted away all threats of an early end to the game, just as a black cloud may be removed from sight by a gentle but persistent breeze. On this last day, however, clouds did materialize - which may have appeared to offer help to the Middlesex bowlers. In fact it is doubtful to my mind whether they did so, nor did they need them. Chasing a commanding total (381 to win in 80 overs, a run rate of 4.76) was too much, and so it proved. Yorkshire were all out just after 3.00 p.m.

Yorkshire are 47 for 2, Lees on strike. He made 62 before becoming Roland-Jones' first victim of the day.

Yorkshire under pressure. Like Middlebrook, the Middlesex spinner Paul Stirling could dance too (1). Having released the ball, all he can do is wait (2). No wicket but some encouragement (3).

LV.com
INSURANCE
LV.com

At appropriate intervals, the ground staff continued their ballet.

Pause at lunch prior to the final act, with many seats in the pavilion vacant. Sunlight and shadow sweep the ground.

Over the four days I moved around the stands, but sat mostly in the Compton Stand, an appropriate place to watch Compton's grandson make 149.

One of the pleasures of Lord's Cricket Ground is the boldness of its architecture.

Gale lbw Dexter 17, ca 1.30. The end is nigh.

The sweep of the architecture is matched by the boldness of the clouds.

Leaning c Robson at first slip,
b Roland-Jones 4.

Roland-Jones bamboozling the Yorkshire batsmen. Ten of the Middlesex team are in the picture.

When this splendid cloud crossed the ground, there were calls from the Yorkshiremen in the crowd, "Bad light, umpires".

The dark cloud has departed, Yorkshire are 117 for 9, and Ryan Sidebottom, last man in, contemplates defeat, momentarily forgetting his three wickets in the first over.

Above: the new way to end a game is for the victors to have a group hug. This is followed by the traditional way (right) where the protagonists shake hands.

Everyone shall have prizes: far away, in front of the pavilion, the losers receive the County Championship trophy, watched by the victors in the game. This elegiac photograph quite fails to capture the drama of the moment when Andy Gale got his hands on the trophy, a ritual triumph denied him in 2014 when Yorkshire won it for the first time in thirteen years. The arcane and murky reasons were to do with abuse Gale gave to Ashwell Prince in a Roses match which the ECB deemed to have been racist and that it was therefore 'inappropriate' for Gale to be involved in the ceremony. (If you want more of this vinegary tale, try searching the internet s.v. Andrew Gale, and more particularly the Cricinfo site: www.espncricinfo.com/county-cricket-2014/content/story/782875.html.)

As I descended from the Compton Stand at the end of the game, I was able to photograph (see bottom left) the junior version on the Lord's Nursery, where the participants were clearly learning to take the game seriously.

"... as the run-stealers flicker to and fro, to and fro,

O my Dexter and my Compton long ago."

Neil Dexter that is, no relation of Ted, and Nick Compton, grandson of Denis.

'Pure pleasure' in the title of this book sounds not only like a 'hackneyed phrase' (see Fowler's Modern English Usage) but the word 'pure' is redundant. Yet while its precise contours have been eroded by overuse, the original shape may be discerned. The author of the idea is Jeremy Bentham (1748-1832) who expounds it in 'An Introduction to the Principles of Morals and Legislation' (1783). Bentham wanted to find a way of calculating the quality and quantity of pleasure that a specific action is likely to cause. The 'circumstances' inherent in an action have to be calculated first, which he summed up in a mnemonic doggerel, the first line of which reads: "Intense, long, certain, speedy, fruitful, pure . . .' So, questions to be answered include how intense the pleasure is, how long it lasts, and so on. The purity of a pleasure is determined by the extent to which it is marred, if at all, by any pain it produces.

This cricket match produced in me a pleasure that was extended over several days, in the quality of the cricket, in the picture of Lord's, in the company I kept, in the sunshine, in the clouds. If the seat was hard (and therefore painful) I did not notice it. If it lacked a glass of wine or two, I only thought of this afterwards. If there was a revenge motif (and therefore distasteful) in Andy Gale lifting the trophy at the end, I was indifferent. What is more, the event was, to use another of Bentham's circumstances, 'fruitful', because sorting out my photographs, writing about the game, and assembling this book has prolonged the pleasure. To describe the whole experience as 'heavenly' sounds trite, but I use the word with meaning: the afterlife might not be dissimilar.

E
W

ABOUT THE AUTHOR

Tim Cawkwell was born in 1948 and lives in Norwich in the United Kingdom. He is the author of several books:

- *The World Encyclopaedia of Film* (co-editor, 1972)
- *Film Past Film Future* (2011)
- *Temenos 2012*, a diary about the Temenos film festival in Greece in 2012
- *From Neuralgistan to the Elated kingdom: a personal journey inside Sicily* (2013)
- *Between Wee Free and Wi Fi: Scotland and the UK belong surely?* (2013)
- *The New Filmgoer's Guide to God* (2014)
- *A Tivoli Companion* (2015)

In 2008 he launched his own website for writing about the cinema, www.timcawkwell.co.uk, which he has regularly maintained ever since, later adding to it a Wordpress blog, www.cawkwell200.com. In 2013 he set up his own imprint, Sforzinda Books, as an outlet for his publishing.

This book can also be made available as a **Photo Book**. This would have a hard cover with a proper spine, and gloss pages which render the images more effectively. However, it would be significantly more expensive than this paperback version, possibly in the region of £70 to £80. If you are interested in obtaining a signed and numbered copy, write to me at 30 Eaton Road, Norwich NR4 6PZ.

Printed in Great Britain
by Amazon